D1567955

FREAKY FISH

Electric Eels

BY THERESA MORLOCK

Gareth Stevens
PUBLISHING

Please visit our website, www.garethstevens.com. For a free color catalog of all our high-quality books, call toll free 1-800-542-2595 or fax 1-877-542-2596.

Cataloging-in-Publication Data

Names: Morlock, Theresa.
Title: Electric eels / Theresa Morlock.
Description: New York : Gareth Stevens Publishing, 2018. | Series: Freaky fish | Includes index.
Identifiers: ISBN 9781538202630 (pbk.) | ISBN 9781538202579 (library bound) | ISBN 9781538203132 (6 pack)
Subjects: LCSH: Electric eel–Juvenile literature.
Classification: LCC QL638.E34 M8417 2018 | DDC 597'.43–dc23

First Edition

Published in 2018 by
Gareth Stevens Publishing
111 East 14th Street, Suite 349
New York, NY 10003

Copyright © 2018 Gareth Stevens Publishing

Designer: Katelyn E. Reynolds
Editor: Joan Stoltman

Photo credits: Cover, pp. 1, 20 Mark Newman/Lonely Planet Images/Getty Images; cover, pp. 1–24 (background) Ensuper/Shutterstock.com; cover, pp. 1–24 (background) macro-vectors/Shutterstock.com; cover, pp. 1–24 (background) Kjpargeter/Shutterstock.com; cover, pp. 1–24 (fact box) nicemonkey/Shutterstock.com; p. 5 Stacey Newman/Shutterstock.com; p. 6 Cuson/Shutterstock.com; p. 7 Bardocz Peter/Shutterstock.com; p. 9 Dominic Salvucci/Flickr.com (Attribution-ShareAlike 2.0 Generic (CC BY-SA 2.0); p. 11 Hein Nouwens/Shutterstock.com; p. 13 © iStockphoto.com/JohnnyMad; p. 15 Billy Hustace/Getty Images; p. 17 Vladimir Wrangel/Shutterstock.com; p. 19 Bigone/Shutterstock.com; p. 21 (light bulb) Davydenko Yuliia/Shutterstock.com; p. 21 (sign) Rashad Ashurov/Shutterstock.com.

All rights reserved. No part of this book may be reproduced in any form without permission in writing from the publisher, except by a reviewer.

Printed in the United States of America

CPSIA compliance information: Batch #CS17GS. For further information contact Gareth Stevens, New York, New York at 1-800-542-2595.

CONTENTS

Words in the glossary appear in **bold** type the first time they are used in the text.

WHAT A SHOCK!

What's so shocking about the electric eel? It can shock, or stun, the animals it hunts with electricity! It can even stun its predators to keep them from attacking. Electric eels can stun with enough electricity to knock down a horse!

Electric eels have about 6,000 special cells in their body called electrocytes (ih-LEHK-truh-syts). Electrocytes produce the electricity that electric eels use to guard themselves or attack. Electric eels also use electricity to navigate, or find their way, through water!

FREAKY FACT!

Electric eels aren't eels at all! Eels have teeth, a fin down their back, breathe through their skin, and spend at least part of their life in salt water. Electric eels don't have or do these things.

4

Electric eels have very bad eyesight, so they use low-level electrical charges to move and find food. This is called electrolocation.

5

A Muddy Home

Electric eels are native to the Orinoco and the Amazon Rivers, two major rivers of South America. They travel through the rivers to streams and ponds and live throughout both rivers' **basins**. Both of these river systems have freshwater, which means they don't have salt.

Electric eels like to make their home in **murky**, slow-moving water where they can blend in with the mud. They live in **shallow** water so they can easily come to the surface to breathe air.

The river basins that electric eels live in are so big they cover most of the northern part of South America!

Orinoco River

Amazon River

SOUTH AMERICA

electric eels

7

A Strange Body

An electric eel can grow 9 feet (2.7 m) long and weigh almost 50 pounds (23 kg)! Most of its **organs** are behind its head. Together, they make up only one-fifth of its body. The rest of it is tail!

An electric eel's body has two poles that its electricity runs between—a positive pole near the head and a negative pole near the tail. It has three special organs along its body that are made up of electrocytes and are used to create electrical charges.

FREAKY FACT!

Even though it's a fish, an electric eel can drown! Electric eels can't breathe in water like other fish do.

Electric eels have to come up to breathe every 10 to 15 minutes because the water is too muddy to give them enough oxygen!

9

It's Electrifying!

An electric eel's special electrical organs are the Sach's organ, main organ, and Hunter's organ. Each emits, or sends out, electrical charges at different voltages. Voltage is how electrical energy is measured. High voltage means that an electrical charge is powerful enough to be harmful. Low voltage means that an electrical charge is weak.

The Sach's organ emits low-voltage charges. The main and Hunter's organs emit very high-voltage charges.

FREAKY FACT!

The electrical charges emitted by an electric eel are called electric organ discharges, or EODs. Electricity that exists inside a living creature is called bioelectricity. The "bio" at the beginning of the word is Greek for "life"!

SACH'S ORGAN

MAIN ORGAN

HUNTER'S ORGAN

The main organ runs from just behind the
electric eel's head to the middle of its tail.
The Hunter's organ runs along the underside of the eel.
The Sach's organ is in the last quarter of the eel.

DINNERTIME!

Electric eels are nocturnal, which means they're active at night! They eat fish, amphibians, and small invertebrates, or animals without backbones, such as crabs and shrimp. To eat a larger creature, they wrap their body around the **prey** to increase the amount of shock their prey receives!

Electric eels can even use their stunning power from a distance, hitting prey with quick **pulses** of electricity. This causes the prey's **muscles** to tighten and freeze. Then the electric eel swallows it whole!

FREAKY FACT!

With the electric eel's powerful electricity, it has few predators in its freshwater **ecosystems**! This means that it's the apex, or top, predator in its home.

An electric eel can stun its prey in just 3 milliseconds! It doesn't have any teeth, but it doesn't need any!

13

Electric Eels in Love

Electric eels send out gentle pulses into the water from their Sach's organ to find **mates**. Once they pair up, the male builds a nest out of his spit for the female to lay eggs in. Gross! And awesome!

Female electric eels lay thousands of eggs, but many will be eaten by predators. Only about 1,200 babies end up **hatching**. The parents stay and guard their young for only a short time after birth, and then the babies are on their own!

FREAKY FACT!

Baby electric eels develop their electric shock organs very early. Even baby electric eels as small as 1.6 inches (4 cm) can shock!

In the wild, electric eels usually live to be about 15 years old.

15

SHOCKING!

Although their electricity might make them seem scary, electric eels aren't usually looking to attack or fight unless they feel **threatened.** They really only use their electric shocks to defend themselves and to catch prey!

It's very rare for people to die from electric eel shocks. However, more than one shock can hurt someone badly! Since our heart uses electrical pulses to work, a few strong shocks from an electric eel might stop your heart! They're best left alone in their murky home in South America.

If you see an electric eel in the wild, don't touch it!

Do Electric Eels Shock Themselves?

It seems electric eels aren't hurt by their own shocks, even though the electricity is all around them in the water after each shock!

Some scientists think it's because the electricity flows through them for such a short time. Others think the eel's brain, heart, and other organs are insulated, or closed off, from the electricity that flows out of and back into the rest of their body. Some scientists even think the eels do get shocked, but are used to it!

FREAKY FACT!

When an electric eel is resting, it can't give off electrical charges. It's only dangerous when it's swimming!

Electric eels have a great sense of hearing. This helps make up for their poor eyesight.

We Need Electric Eels

Electric eels are important members of their ecosystems. As apex predators, they're key to keeping prey animals in check. Without them, prey animals would overtake the area and eat so much they'd harm the ecosystem! Electric eels also help out by recycling nutrients, which all living things need to grow and stay alive.

From their shocking navigation abilities to their electrifying hunting methods, electric eels are certainly freaky fish! Their powerful, strange skills show just how cool nature can be!

FREAKY FAST FACTS!

Even after they die, electric eels' bodies can keep shocking for up to 8 hours!

A very large electric eel can produce enough electricity for 12 lightbulbs!

Electric eels are one of about 500 species, or kinds, of fish that produce electricity!

Electric eels give off little pulses of 10 volts while they're swimming to navigate the muddy waters they call home!

A person can survive a shock from an electric eel!

GLOSSARY

basin: an area that draws off water from surrounding land

ecosystem: all the living things in an area

hatch: to break open or come out of

mate: one of two animals that come together to produce babies, or to come together to make babies

muscle: one of the parts of the body that allow movement

murky: dark and gloomy

organ: a part inside an animal's body

prey: an animal that is hunted by other animals for food

pulse: a brief change in an amount of electricity

shallow: not deep

threatened: in danger

FOR MORE INFORMATION

BOOKS

Lawrence, Ellen. *Electric Eel.* New York, NY: Bearport Publishing, 2017.

Roza, Greg. *Zap! The Electric Eel and Other Electric Animals.* New York, NY: PowerKids Press, 2011.

Van Dyck, Sara. *Electric Eels.* Minneapolis, MN: Lerner Publications, 2008.

WEBSITES

Animals: Electric Eel
kids.nationalgeographic.com/animals/electric-eel
Read fun facts about electric eels!

Electric Eel
aqua.org/explore/animals/electric-eel
Read all the key information about the electric eel on the National Aquarium's website!

Ology Cards: Electric Eel
amnh.org/explore/ology/ology-cards/121-electric-eel
Flip the card to learn all about the electric eel!

Publisher's note to educators and parents: Our editors have carefully reviewed these websites to ensure that they are suitable for students. Many websites change frequently, however, and we cannot guarantee that a site's future contents will continue to meet our high standards of quality and educational value. Be advised that students should be closely supervised whenever they access the Internet.

INDEX